# Polka Dot Girls

*Designed. Original. Treasured.*

By
Kristie Kerr & Paula Yarnes

Copyright 2011 Kristie Kerr and Paula Yarnes. All Rights Reserved.

No part of this book may be reproduced, transmitted, or utilized in any form or by any means,graphic, electronic or mechanical, including photocopying, recording, taping, or by any information storage or retrieval, without the permission in writing from the publisher. WITH THE EXCEPTION OF THE POLKA DOT PLUS WEEKLY CHALLENGES, TAKE HOME ACTIVITY SHEETS AND PARENT PARTNERS, WHICH MAY BE DUPLICATED FOR GROUP USE ONLY.

Unless otherwise indicated, all Scripture quotations are taken from the Holy Bible, New Living Translation, copyright © 1996, 2004, 2007 by Tyndale House Foundation. Used by permission of Tyndale House Publishers, Inc., Carol Stream, Illinois 60188. All rights reserved.

THE HOLY BIBLE, NEW INTERNATIONAL VERSION®, NIV® Copyright © 1973, 1978, 1984, 2011 by Biblica, Inc.™ Used by permission. All rights reserved worldwide.

Scripture taken from The Message. Copyright © 1993, 1994, 1995, 1996, 2000, 2001, 2002. Used by permission of NavPress Publishing Group.

Scripture taken from the Contemporary English Version © 1991, 1992, 1995 by American Bible Society, Used by Permission.

Scripture taken from the New Century Version®. Copyright © 2005 by Thomas Nelson, Inc. Used by permission. All rights reserved.

Scripture taken from the Common English Bible P.O. Box 801 201 Eighth Avenue South Nashville, TN 37202-0801

ISBN: 987-0-9840312-9-0

Printed in the United States of America

1st Printing

# Contents

**Getting to Know Him** .................. **1-22**
    Lesson ............................ 1
    My Polka Dot Spot ................ 8
    Polka Dot Project ................ 15
    Polka Dot Plus
        Activity Sheets .............. 19
        Weekly Challenge ............ 21

**God the Father** ...................... **23-42**
    Lesson ............................ 23
    My Polka Dot Spot ................ 29
    Polka Dot Project ................ 36
    Polka Dot Plus
        Activity Sheets .............. 39
        Weekly Challenge ............ 41

**God the Son** ........................ **43-58**
    Lesson ............................ 43
    My Polka Dot Spot ................ 48
    Polka Dot Project ................ 53
    Polka Dot Plus
        Activity Sheets .............. 54
        Weekly Challenge ............ 57

**God the Holy Spirit** .................. **59-73**
    Lesson ............................ 59
    My Polka Dot Spot ................ 64
    Polka Dot Project ................ 69
    Polka Dot Plus
        Activity Sheets .............. 70
        Weekly Challenge ............ 73

# Dedication

**Dedicated to the girls who inspire us:**

**Anja** who does funny accents...

**JoJo** who DEFIES ALL ODDS...

**Catelyn** who is a SURVIVOR...

**Lucy** who LOVES unconditionally...

**Betty** who LIGHTS UP THE ROOM...

**Dottie** who loves tutus AND FISHING POLES...

**Meg** who is so funny she could possibly be the next Lucille Ball...

**Ling** who is NOT AFRAID to speak her mind...

**Natalie** who can organize like nobody's business...

**Jeorgia** who has AMAZING COURAGE...

and **Lily** who is simply sweet!

**You amaze us.**
**Go change the world.**

# Knowing God

week 1

## Getting to Know Him

WHAT'S THE POINT?
GOD KNOWS EVERYTHING ABOUT YOU,
AND HE WANTS YOU TO KNOW EVERYTHING ABOUT HIM.

### theme verse

*The Lord is close to all who call on Him.*
Psalm 145:18

### related bible story

Exodus 4:1-17

Do you have a best friend? What is her name? How do you know her? Why is she your friend?

Have you ever met somebody and thought to yourself right away, "I want to be her friend?" You look at her and she seems so nice or fun or smart and you just want to know more about her?

I had a friend once named Sarah. I met her at school, and she made me laugh. She was very nice to people and wore pretty shoes. I knew right away that I wanted to be Sarah's friend. So, I started talking to her. I asked her about the things that she liked. The amazing thing was that she liked the same things I liked!

She liked chocolate ice cream cones and puppies and playing school and hated wearing dresses. Just like me! And the more time I spent with Sarah, the more I learned about her… and the more I liked her. She was a very good friend.

And you know what? It's the same way with God. Sometimes it can seem like God is great big and far away. It can feel like He is just way to big to care about something as little as me. But the truth is, God wants to be your friend!

Isn't that crazy! The great big God who made all the stars and oceans and makes the snow fall from heaven wants to be friends with **YOU**!

*O Lord, You are the friend of your worshippers…* – Psalm 25:10 (CEV)

God already knows EVERYTHING about you. He knows what you're thinking, what you're feeling, what you are going to do today, and even what you are going to do tomorrow! The Bible tells us that He even knows how many hairs you have on your head!

I Peter 1:2 says, *God the Father knew you and chose you long ago.* Not only does He know everything about you, but He CHOSE you to be His friend! Imagine the coolest, smartest, most amazing person in the universe deciding that out of all the people in the entire world – they wanted to be friends with you. That's pretty amazing to me!

God knows you. God loves you. And God wants you to know Him too.

So, how do you get to know God better? The same way I got to know my friend Sarah. By discovering what He is like. By spending time together. By learning about the things that are important to Him. By finding out what He cares about.

God knows everything about you, and He wants you to know everything about Him.

Polka Dot Girls ❀ Knowing God

week 1

**There are 3 ways we can get to know God better!**

# ➡ 1. Reading The Bible

The Bible is a letter from God to you! God had LOTS of things that He wanted to say to you. He wanted to tell you about Himself. He wanted to tell you about things He had done for other people. He wanted to give you instructions on how you could live your life in a way that would make Him happy.

*I have hidden your word in my heart, that I might not sin against you.* – Psalm 119:11 NLT

So, He gave us the Bible. He told some people many, many years ago to write down some very special stories and words that would help you and me be able to understand Him better. And now, you and I can read the Bible and learn what God is like!

You can read the stories and see how God helped people. You can see how He told them to live. You can learn about His heart and how He thinks and most importantly how very, very much He loves you.

My friend Emily was facing something difficult and she didn't know what to do. She had to get up in front of her whole class and give a book report. Emily was *Scared to Death* of talking in front of people. Her knees would shake and her hands would get sweaty and her tummy wouldn't feel so good. What was she going to do?

She opened her Bible one day, and found a story about a man named Moses. God asked Moses to lead His people out of a really bad situation. He was to go before the Pharoah, who was the King of Egypt and tell him to let God's people go. Moses was SCARED! He did not want to stand in front of the King. I can imagine that his knees would shake and his hands would get sweaty and his tummy wouldn't feel so good… just like Emily.

But, here is what God said to Moses. *When you speak, I will be with you and give you the words to say.* – Exodus 4:12 CEV

WHOA! That is exactly what Emily needed to hear. It was so cool to see that the words that God had said to Moses in the Bible could be so helpful to Emily. She wrote the words on a little card and carried it with her the days before she had to give her speech. When the day finally came, she read the card one more time, took a deep breath, and got up in front of the class confident that God was with her and that He would help her do her very best.

The Bible is FULL of stories just like this one that can help us get through the things we face in our lives. It has all kinds of wisdom and special help for us. There are so many times when I open up my Bible and find a verse that totally encourages me.

WHO KNEW?

The name "Moses" means "drawn out" because he was drawn out of the water. God wants you to draw closer to Him by reading the Bible, talking to Him, and going to church.

God uses the Bible to speak to us, but it also tells us what God is like. We learn that He is faithful. Hosea 2:20 says, *I will be faithful to you and make you mine.* We can know, by reading the Bible, that God will never let us down.

We learn that God is perfect. He never makes mistakes. He never changes. We can know that He will love us the same today as He did yesterday and will love us just as much tomorrow.

The Bible is God's letter to you. It's important that you read it everyday so that you can learn more and more what God is like. That is how you get closer to him!

Polka Dot Girls ❦ Knowing God

week 1

**The second way we can know God better is:**

## ➔ 2. By Talking to God

Have you ever had a really long talk with a good friend? Maybe you have had a sleepover at your house with your best friend and you have laid in bed talking about what you want to be when you grow up, or your favorite movie or maybe even what you're afraid of.

I don't know about you, but when I talk to my friends something really cool happens between us. I feel closer to that person. I feel better about the things I'm going through. I know that I'm not alone and that there is someone who wants to hear the things that I care about.

And God wants us to talk to Him just like we talk to one of our friends. Actually, "praying" to God is really just talking to God! He wants you to come to Him with the things that are bothering you. He wants you to tell Him the things you are excited about and what you are thankful for. He loves it when you share your heart with Him.

And something will happen to your heart when you tell God your thoughts, worries, and problems. You will begin to feel closer to Him just like you do when you are talking to your friends! It's so nice to know that He cares about the things that you care about. He is *Always* listening – and is the best friend you could ever want to have!

And not only can you talk to God, but God will talk to you!

*Ask me, and I will tell you remarkable secrets...* – Jeremiah 33:3 NLT

You may not hear His voice out loud like you hear your Mom or Dad, but God whispers to your heart. When God speaks to me, it's like I hear words in my head that I know weren't my own idea. I always try to write down the words that I feel God is speaking to my heart so that I can remember what He is saying to me. And the amazing thing is that when God speaks to you, it will ALWAYS line up with what the Bible says! So, whenever I hear Him speak, I go to my Bible and find verses that confirm what He has said to my heart.

God will give you answers to your problems. He will challenge you to do better with your attitude or behavior. He will make you feel better when you're sad or upset. He will talk to you about your future. If you will listen, God will speak to you.

One of my ALL TIME favorite verses in the Bible is Psalm 27:8. It says, *My heart has heard you say, "Come and talk with me.* And my heart responds, 'Lord, I am coming.' This verse makes me imagine God, calling my name and saying, "Hey Kristie... come on over here and sit down and tell me about your day. What's going on? How are you doing?" I imagine myself sitting right next to God just talking to Him about everything. It makes me feel so close to Him when we have those times together.

### POLKA DOT POINTERS

Get a cute journal that you can draw a picture or write down things that God says to you. Write down your prayers and then make sure to go back and write down when God answers them. Write out verses that you read in the Bible that speak to you, and take note of the special things you feel God whisper to your heart.

**And the last way we can grow closer to God is to:**

## ➡ 3. Go to church.

Every morning, you wake up, comb your hair, brush your teeth, put on your clothes and do what? GO TO SCHOOL! How many of you like school?!

Why do you go to school every day? To learn! You go to school so that you can learn about reading and science and math. There are teachers there that show you how to do things. You can discover all kinds of new ideas by listening to your teachers.

Polka Dot Girls ❦ Knowing God

week 1

Church is a place where you can learn more about God! You will hear stories about the things He has done in the past. You will learn about the things in the Bible. You will learn the things that make God happy and the things that He doesn't want you to do. (You will make lots of great friends and have a lot of fun too!!)

It's important that you read your Bible and talk to God when you are at home. But there is something really amazing that happens when you come together with other people who believe in God like you do and learn about Him. It helps you grow stronger in your faith. You can talk to your teachers and your Christian friends about God. You can ask questions about the things you are unsure about. You can have people pray for you and your family.

Make sure that you come to church regularly! It's important to spend time with other people who believe in God like you do!

God knows everything about you, and He wants you to know everything about Him.

**Closing Prayer:** *Dear God, thank you that you know me. Thank you that you want to be my very best friend. I want to know more and more about you too. Help me to spend time reading the Bible, talking to you, and learning more about you at church. Thank you for choosing me to be your friend. Amen.*

# My Polka Dot Spot

It's so much fun getting to know people better! We can learn more about our friends by spending time with them, talking to them, and by learning about the things they like to do! Write three things you know about your closest friends.

God wants to be your friend! He wants you to know everything about Him. In the lesson, we talked about three ways we could grow closer to God. Do you remember what they are? Write them out here.

week 1

Do you think there is a difference between KNOWING ABOUT someone and actually KNOWING them?

Who is your FAVORITE celebrity? It can be an athlete, a singer, a person in movies or TV! Write their name here and three things you know about them.

So you know a lot ABOUT them – but do you really KNOW them?

Now, who is your best friend? Write their name here and three things you know about them.

Now, look at the list below and check the box if it applies:

### CELEBRITY          BFE

☐  you actually talk to this person  ☐

☐  you spend time with them  ☐

☐  you can call + talk anytime  ☐

☐  they know lots of stuff about you!  ☐

Polka Dot Girls ❀ Knowing God

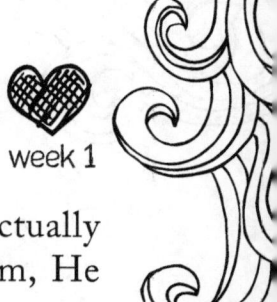

week 1

There's a big difference between knowing ABOUT someone and actually KNOWING them. God doesn't want you to just know ABOUT Him, He wants to actually KNOW you!

Reading the Bible is one of the VERY best ways we can learn about God! Below you will find 3 scripture verses that talk about how important it is to spend time reading God's Word. Use your Bible to look up the verses and write them down in the space provided.

Psalm 119:11:

Psalm 119:105:

2 Timothy 3:16-17:

Do you ever talk to God? He loves it when we spend time telling Him what we're thinking about. On the letter below, write a letter to God about some things going on in your life right now.

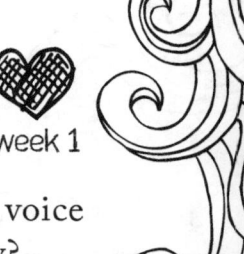
week 1

Have you ever felt like God has talked to you? You may not have heard is voice out loud, but maybe you felt him speaking in your heart. What did he say?

We learn LOTS of things about God by coming to church! On the picture below, write out some of the things you have learned about God by spending time in His house!

Our theme verse this week is Psalm 145:18. Write it out in the space below and then see if you can memorize it!

Polka Dot Girls ❦ Knowing God

week 1

## "I Know God" Book

Supplies Needed:

- Key words on page 17
- Bibles (to look up verses)
- 3 sheets of 8 x 11 pretty paper per
  Cut the three sheets in half, so you have 6 sheets of paper. One for the cover and five for the pages of the book.
- Glue
- Scissors
- Stapler
- Markers
- Stickers, embellishments, glitter, etc.

Prep:

1. Put together the six sheets of pretty paper.
2. Staple the pretty paper three times on the left side to make a book.
3. Cut out the words provided on page 17

What should I do?

Each of the verses listed below highlight a particular attribute of God.

- Look up the verses in the Bible and name the key word that describes God.
- Once you have figured out the key word, cut it out and glue it into your "I Know God" book.
- Make a title page and decorate the pages with stickers, embellishments and other pretty things.

Keywords for Polka Dot Project:

God is **LOVE**

**1 John 4:8** – *But anyone who does not love does not know God, for **God is love**.*

God is **KIND**

**Psalm 116:5** – *How **kind** the Lord is! How good he is! So merciful, this God of ours!*

God **KNOWS EVERYTHING**

**Psalm 139:1** – *O Lord, you have examined my heart and **know everything** about me.*

God **NEVER CHANGES**

**Hebrews 13:8** – *Jesus Christ **is the same** yesterday, today, and forever.*

God is **PATIENT**

**Romans 2:4** – *Don't you see how wonderfully kind, tolerant, and **patient** God is with you?*

week 1

## Activity Sheet

In the space provided, draw a picture of you and your closest friend.

God wants to be your closest friend! He knows everything about you, and wants you to know everything about Him.

The verses below talk about knowing God. Look up each verse in your Bible and find the common word. Fill in the blank. All scripture NIV.

**Psalm 9:10** – *Those who _____ your name trust in you, for you, O lord, do not abandon those who search for you.*

**Psalm 119:168** – *Yes, I obey your commandments and laws because you _____ everything I do.*

**Psalm 139:23** – *Search me, O God, and _____ my heart.*

**Daniel 11:32** – *But the people who _____ their God will be strong and will resist him.*

**John 10:27** – *My sheep listen to my voice; I _____ them, and they follow me.*

**Phil 3:8** – *Yes, everything else is worthless when compared with the infinite value of _____ ing Christ Jesus my Lord. For his sake, I have discarded everything else, counting it all as garbage, so that I could gain Christ and become one with him.*

**Phil 3:10** – *I want to _____ Christ and experience the mighty power that raised him from the dead.*

**Col 1:10** – *All the while, you will grow as you learn to _____ God better and better.*

Polka Dot Girls ❀ Knowing God

week 1

## Weekly Challenge

**Grow** – GROW your faith by reading the following Bible Story: **Exodus 4:1-17**

**Love** – Show God's LOVE this week by making a card for a friend or family member.

**Act** – Take ACTION: Do ONE thing to help you know God better. Talk to God about something you're worried or excited about. Go to church. Next week, share with your group what you did!

**Memorize** – MEMORIZE the theme verse for this week.

*The Lord is close to all who call on Him.*
– Psalm 145:18

# Knowing God

*week 2*

## God the Father

**WHAT'S THE POINT?**

**GOD IS OUR HEAVENLY FATHER.
HE LOVES US,
PROTECTS US,
AND PROVIDES FOR US.**

### theme verse

*See how much our Father loves us,
for he calls us his children, and that is what we are!*
1 John 3:1

### related bible story

Exodus 16:1-31

In the last lesson, we talked about the fact that God knows everything about you – and that He wants you to know everything about Him. We talked about how we can learn more about God.

Today we're going to talk some more about what God is like.

One of the most amazing things about God is that there are three different parts to who God is. Let me show you what I mean.

I want you to think about three things: water, ice, and steam. What do all three things have in common? They're all made of the same thing - water!

Water can be in liquid form – like when it comes out of the faucet in your kitchen or the hose in your back yard. You can drink it on a hot day. You can take a shower or bath and get cleaned up. You can put it on your flowers and it will help them grow.

But if you took water in liquid form and put it in your freezer for a few hours… something cool would happen to it. It would turn into ice! It's still water – but just different.

And then what if you took some water and put it on the stove and heated it up? It would start boiling and eventually turn into a vapor that would float into the air called steam.

God is the same way! There are three parts to Him. They are all different forms, but they are all the same thing. The same way we have water, ice and steam – we have God the Father, God the Son or Jesus and God the Holy Spirit. They are one, but different. We call this the Trinity–one God in three different parts.

Over the next few chapters, we are going to talk about the three different parts of God – the Father, Son, and Holy Spirit. We're going to learn about each one of them and what makes them different and special.

So, today we're going to start by talking about God the Father.

I think it's really, really cool that God calls himself our "Father." Cause fathers are really, really special.

Amber loves to spend time with her Dad. They have a lot in common, especially when it comes to the outdoors. They both love to be outside, go camping, and ride their bikes. Every year, they take a trip to a special camping spot, just the two of them. They set up their tents, build their campfires and spend a whole week hiking, fishing, and spending time together.

Amber absolutely loves the time with her dad. She always knows that he is going to make sure she is safe. He watches over her and keeps her away from anything dangerous or scary. Sometimes at night, she will hear a strange noise and she will start to get scared. But as soon as she remembers that her Dad is there with her, she isn't scared anymore because she knows that he is there protecting her.

week 2

# AND GOD THE FATHER IS THE SAME WAY WITH YOU AND ME.

## ⇒ 1. God is our PROTECTOR

He is always watching over us, protecting us and keeping us safe from danger and harm. Psalm 121:7-8 gives us a really cool picture of how God protects us. It says, *"The Lord keeps you from all harm and watches over your life. The Lord keeps watch over you as you come and go, both now and forever."*

God is always watching over you. In those moments when you feel afraid of something, you can be sure that God is right there with you, keeping you safe. You don't have to be scared or ever, ever, ever feel like you are alone. God is watching over you. He is our protector.

What is a protector? Well, it's like a shield in front of us.

Imagine someone was throwing snowballs or water balloons at you (FUN!) when suddenly one of your friends jumps in front of you and blocks the things being thrown at you. When they were standing in front of you – no one could hit you with anything! They protected you by being a shield.

God is YOUR shield! He stands before you and around you and keeps you safe. Psalm 27:1 says, *"The Lord is my light and my salvation – so why should I be afraid? The Lord is my fortress, protecting me from danger, so why should I tremble?"* You don't ever have to be afraid, because you can know that God is watching over you and will protect you from harm.

Another great thing about Amber's trips with her dad is that He makes sure she has everything she needs. He packs the cooler with lots of yummy things for them to eat. He catches the fish that they cook over the fire and eat for dinner. He makes sure she has clothes that are warm enough and shoes that will keep her feet safe and dry. He bought her a new sleeping bag that is extra warm for the nights when it gets cold outside. Amber never has to worry, because she knows that her Dad will provide everything she needs.

**And God the Father is the same way with you and me.**

## 2. God is our PROVIDER

Everything you and I have, has been given to us by God the Father. I know it may seem like your mom or dad or grandma bought you all the things you need. But the Bible tells us that everything we have has come from Him. He provides a job for your mom and dad so they can earn money to buy you things. He makes sure that you have the things you need every single day.

There is a story in Exodus chapter 16 which tells us about God providing for His people. The Israelites had just escaped the land of Egypt and now were on a journey to a new place to live. They were in the desert and there was nothing to eat. They were so hungry and they wondered what they were going to do.

So they prayed to God, and he did something amazing. In the morning, when they got out of their tents and went outside, there was food covering the ground called "manna." Every morning, the manna would fall from heaven and the people would gather it and eat it. God provided food for them every single day!

God is your provider. He provides your food, clothes, toys, and games. He makes sure that you have all the things you need. Sometimes we can worry about things, but it's important to remember that God will always provide for you.

Matthew 6:25-27 says this: *That is why I tell you not to worry about everyday life – whether you have enough food and drink, or enough clothes to wear. Isn't life more than food, and your body more than clothing? Look at the birds. They don't plant or harvest or store food in barns, for your heavenly Father feeds them. And aren't you far more valuable to him that they are? Can all your worries add a single moment to your life?*

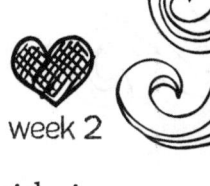

Did you catch that? God is even making sure that the birds you see outside in the trees have enough food and a place to live. And God cares WAY more for you than for the birds!! He will always make sure you are taken care of. That is His job as your Heavenly Father.

Our friend Amber loves her dad so much. He is a really, really good Dad. He spends time with her and helps her learn lots of things and he really, really loves her. But you know what? Sometimes her Dad makes mistakes. Sometimes He gets frustrated and says something that hurts her feelings. Sometimes he has to work a lot and cannot be there for her when she really needs someone to talk to. As much as Amber's dad loves her, he is still human, and he makes mistakes.

And that is why it is so important that we know God as our Heavenly Father. You know why?

## ⇒ 3. Because God the Father is PERFECT

God is like our earthly Fathers in SO many ways, but there is one way that He is absolutely different. God the Father doesn't EVER make mistakes. He ALWAYS does the right thing and He ALWAYS does what is best for you.

See, no matter how much your Mom and Dad love you, they are still people just like you and me. And people make mistakes. How many of you here have ever made a mistake? How many of you have every said or done something that hurt another person's feelings? How many of you have ever done something that you wish you could take back? All of us have, because we are humans – and humans are NOT perfect.

But God is not human. He is God. He never, ever, ever makes a mistake. That makes me feel so SAFE! I can know that no matter what, God will love me perfectly, treat me perfectly, and do the absolute best thing for me every time. I don't ever have to wonder if God forgot about me or is mad at me or doesn't love me anymore. He will never ever let me down. He will never ever fail me. He will never ever do anything that isn't **PERFECT**.

> **JUST SO YOU KNOW:**
>
> Some girls don't have a dad in their life. There are lots of reasons that this may be the case. You should know that it is **NEVER** your fault if you don't have a dad who is close to you. It must be really hard sometimes to wish you had a dad like other girls. But you should know that God promises that He will be the very best Father you could ever imagine. There is even a verse in the Bible **JUST** for you. It says in Psalm 68:5, *A father to the fatherless, a defender of widows, is God in His holy dwelling.* You may not have a father here on earth, or maybe you do have a father but you are not close to him. God will step in and be the best father you ever dreamed of having. It's His promise to you.

God is your Heavenly Father. He loves you so much. You are His most precious daughter and He thinks you are amazing. Whenever you are scared, think of your Heavenly Father standing before you, protecting you and keeping you safe. When you're worried about something, remember that He is your Father who will give you everything you need. And when you need to know that you can count on someone to always be there for you, you can count on your perfect, unchanging Father God.

**Closing Prayer:** *God, thank you for being my Father. It makes me feel so special and safe to know that you are taking care of me. Help me to always remember that I am your daughter and that you love me. Amen.*

In this lesson, we learned that God is one God in three different parts... something we call the Trinity. Color in the names of the three parts of God.

# God the Father

# God the Son (Jesus)

# God the Holy Spirit

God the Father is our Protector. What does it mean to PROTECT someone?

Draw a picture of yourself that shows how you feel knowing that God is always watching over you.

Polka Dot Girls ❖ Knowing God

God the Father is our provider. What does it mean to PROVIDE for someone?

week 2

There is a big difference between things you NEED and things you WANT. In the left column, list some things that you NEED. In the right column, list some things that you WANT.

It's important to remember that God promises to provide the things that we need. That doesn't mean that we get everything we WANT. BUT – sometimes God blesses us by giving us the things we NEED and some of the things we want. That is why we should be so thankful for the things we have... because God gave them to us!

Polka Dot Girls ❦ Knowing God

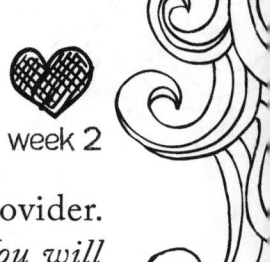

There is a really cool verse in the Bible about God being our provider. 2 Corinthians 9:8 says, *"And God will generously provide all you need. You will always have everything you need and plenty left over to share with others."* What do you think this verse means?

Write out the first part of this verse three times: *"And God will generously provide all you need."* – 2 Corinthians 9:8. See if you can memorize it!

What does it mean to be "PERFECT?"

Do you know anyone who is perfect?

No! Only God is perfect. All of us make mistakes, but God NEVER does. God is perfect!

week 2

It's so cool to know that God is perfect… no matter what He will never, ever let us down. Write a letter to God thanking Him for being the perfect Father.

# "God is my Shield" Wall Hanging

Supplies Needed:
- Template of Shield on page 37
- Cardstock (white or colored)
- Scissors
- 3-Hole Punch
- Ribbon
- Crayons and markers
- Foam shapes, stickers, sparkles and pretty embellishments

Prep:
- Glue shield template onto white or favorite color cardstock.
- Cut out the shield.

What should I do?

1. Glue your shield onto cardstock.
2. Cut out the shield.
3. Punch holes around the shield.
3. Thread ribbon through the holes beginning from the top and ending at the top.
4. Leave enough ribbon at the beginning and the end to tie into a ribbon.
5. Decorate shield with crayons, markers and embellishments.
6. On the back of the shield write down the theme verse for this week.
7. Hang in your room!

Polka Dot Girls ❧ Knowing God

week 2

## Activity Sheet

God is the Best Father EVER! Next to each letter of the word FATHER write down an attribute that describes what a great FATHER God is.

**F** _____

**A** _____

**T** _____

**H** _____

**E** _____

**R** _____

**Examples:** Friend, Holy, etc.

Look up the verses below, write in the missing words in the blank spaces. All scripture NIV.

**Psalm 2:7** – The Lord said to me, *You are my son. Today I have become your* _____.

**Psalm 89:26** – And he will call out to me, *You are my* _____, *my God, and the* _____ *of my salvation.*

**Isaiah 9:6** – *And He will be called: Wonderful* _____, *Mighty God, Everlasting* _____, *Prince of Peace.*

**Matthew 5:16** – *In the same way, let your good* _____ *shine out for all to see, so that everyone will praise your heavenly* _____.

**Romans 8:15-16** – *So you have not received a spirit that makes you fearful* _____. *Instead, you received God's Spirit when he adopted you as his own* _____. *Now we call him, 'Abba* _____.' *For His spirit joins with our spirit to affirm that we are God's children.*

**2 Cor 6:18** – *And I will be your* _____, *and you will be my sons and* _____, *says the Lord Almighty.*

Polka Dot Girls ❀ Knowing God

week 2

## Weekly Challenge

**Grow** – Grow your faith by reading the following Bible Story: **2 Corinthians 9:6-9**

**Love** – Show God's love this week by doing a simple act of service for a neighbor or friend outside your family.

**Act** – God is your heavenly Father. You are his child. God planned for you to be born. Talk to your mom and dad about the day you were born. In your journal, write down interesting facts about the day you were born. (date, time, place, weather) Then write down what you think you mean to Him? Thank God for planning you and giving you life! Next week, share with your group about the things you learned about the day you were born.

**Memorize** – Memorize the theme verse for this week.

*See how much our Father loves us,*
*for he calls us his children, and that is what we are!*

– 1 John 3:1

# Knowing God

week 3

## God the Son (Jesus)

### What's the Point?

JESUS CAME TO EARTH AND DIED ON THE CROSS TO GIVE US AN "ALL ACCESS" PASS TO GOD.

### theme verse

*"So now we can rejoice in our wonderful new relationship with God because our Lord Jesus Christ has made us friends of God."*

Romans 5:11

### related bible story

*Sin Enters the World*

Genesis 3

Jesus is God's son. He was in heaven with the Father and the Holy Spirit, but there was a problem with people on the earth that God had created. How many of you have heard the story of Adam and Eve?

Adam and Eve were the first people that God ever created. Genesis 1 tells us God created man and gave them one rule. They were **NOT** to eat the fruit from a certain tree in the garden. But Adam and Eve did not follow the rules that God gave them, and the moment that they disobeyed God, **SIN** entered the world. Sin is not just the things that you and I do that are wrong – sin became a part of who we are. We are just imperfect people who have a part of us that is sinful.

How many of you have baby brothers or sisters? How many of you have watched your younger brothers and sisters say "MINE" and get kind of mean? How many of you have had your baby brothers or sisters hit you or be selfish? Now, my question is: Who taught them to be naughty? Did you teach your little sister to be mean? Did your mom and dad sit them down and tell them that they should scream and cry when they don't get their own way? NO! They were just born that way? And you and I were too.

Each and every one of us was born with a sinful nature. The Bible tells us this in Romans 3:23. It says, *"For everyone has sinned; we all fall short of God's glorious standard."* Every one of us makes mistakes, does the wrong thing, and thinks only about ourselves. It doesn't mean that we are bad – it just means that we are born imperfect. We are born with a sinful nature.

But GOD is PERFECT. He doesn't have a sinful nature like you and me. He never does the wrong thing. He has never sinned. He is perfect. And because He is perfect and holy, He cannot be around sin. He just can't.

God loved you SO much that He wanted to find a way to be close to you and me – even though our nature was sinful. And this is where Jesus comes in. John 3:16 says, *"For God so loved the world so much that He gave His one and only son, so that everyone who believes in Him will not perish but have eternal life."*

Jesus is God's son. He is perfect and sinless just like God the Father. So God came up with a plan. Jesus would come down to earth as a person – just like you and me. He would be fully God and yet fully human. And He would live a perfect life… without sinning at all. Who knows how Jesus came to earth? What holiday do we celebrate when Jesus came down to earth? That's right – Christmas! Jesus came down to earth as a little baby born in a manger on Christmas!

Jesus came to earth for a very important reason. The only way that God could be close to you and me is if Jesus died on the cross and rose again. If He did that, then there

Polka Dot Girls ❀ Knowing God

would be a way for us to have a close relationship with God – even though we are sinful people. And so that is exactly what He did.

Jesus came to earth, grew up and became a man and lived a sinless life. And then when He was 33 years old, He died on the cross. But three days after He died, He rose again! And then He went back up into heaven to be with the Father once again.

When he did that, something amazing happened. Now we have a way to be close to God. Even though we are sinful people, because of what Jesus did on the cross, you and I now can have a relationship with God! Isn't that amazing!

**WHO KNEW?**

Another name that we sometimes use to talk about Jesus is Emmanuel.

It means "God is with Us."

There was a girl named Stacy who went to a concert of her absolutely favorite singer ever. She was crazy about this girl and could hardly wait to get to the show. After the show was over, she noticed people walking through a door that said "Backstage Access." She wondered what was back there and so she walked closer to get a better look. On the other side of the door, she saw the singer… HER singer standing backstage!!! Stacy could hardly believe what she was seeing!! She saw other people walking through the door, so she walked over, crazy excited that she was going to get the chance to meet her!

But the security guard at the door stopped her and said, "I'm sorry, but you can't go back there without one of these." He held up a lanyard that had a little card on the bottom that said "All Access." She was so disappointed. She knew that her absolute favorite, favorite, favorite singer was right behind that door and if she could just get through then she would be able to meet her and get to know her and spend time with her. But she couldn't get through that door without the "All Access" pass.

Then all of the sudden, a woman walked up beside her and smiled. She held up something in her hand. Stacy could hardly believe it… it was an ALL ACCESS PASS!!!! The nice woman looked at her and said, "Would you like to have this pass?"

Would she like to have this pass?!?!? Are you kidding me? Of COURSE she wanted the pass! Like CRAZY wanted the pass! With that pass she could spend time with the most amazingly awesome person in the universe!!!!!

She could hardly get the words out of her mouth. "YES! I would love to have the pass! Thank you so much!!" The woman placed the lanyard around her neck and Stacy walked through the door and got to meet her favorite singer.

And that is exactly what Jesus did for you and me. We were separated from God. We couldn't be close to Him because of our sinful nature. There was a big door between us and Him. But when Jesus came to earth and died on the cross, He made a way for you and me to have an "All Access" pass to God. We can have a relationship with Him. We can know Him. We can be close to Him. Through Jesus, we can be forgiven of all those sinful things we do!

So – how do we get that All Access pass to God? We simply ask Jesus for it! We ask Him to come into our lives and forgive us for all the things we've done wrong and ask Jesus to come and live in our hearts. When we ask Jesus into our lives, He places a big "All Access" pass around our necks. We are forgiven of our sins and now can have a close, personal relationship with God. Romans 5:11 says, "*So now we can rejoice in our wonderful new relationship with God because our Lord Jesus Christ has made us friends of God.*"

The whole reason that Jesus came to earth and died for you and me was simply because He loved us SO very much. He wanted to be close to you so He provided a way. Aren't you so thankful that Jesus died on the cross for you?

Maybe some of you have never asked Jesus to come into your hearts and today you want to ask Him to forgive you of your sins and put a big "All Access" pass around your neck. Today you can invite Jesus into your life and begin living your life in a close, personal relationship with Him.

Polka Dot Girls ❀ Knowing God

week 3

Jesus would LOVE to have a relationship with you. He died on the cross because He loved you so much and today you can ask Him to come into your heart. If you would like to do that today, all you have to do is pray this prayer and begin living your life for Him.

**Closing prayer:** *"Dear Jesus, I thank you that you came to earth and died on the cross. Please forgive me for all my sins and come into my life. I want to live for you, and I want to spend time getting to know you more so that I can be closer to you. Thank you for coming into my heart. Amen."*

Adam and Eve were the first two people that God created. What was the one thing that God told them they could not do?

What did Adam and Eve do?

What happened when Adam and Eve disobeyed God?

week 3

Have you ever done anything bad? Have you ever disobeyed your Mom or Dad or hurt someone? That shows us that we have are all born with a sinful nature! Write out the verse below three times.

*"There is no one who always does what is right, not even one."* —Romans 3:10 (NCV)

Because we are all sinful, there is a door between us and God. BUT – someone made a way for us to be able to walk through the door. Who did that for us? Write His name on the door and color it in with happy colors because this is GOOD NEWS!!!

How did Jesus make a way for us to have access to God the Father?

week 3

Look up John 14:6. On the picture of the cross below, write in the three words that are used to describe Jesus in this verse.

YOU can have an all access pass to God by asking Jesus to come into your heart. Have you ever done that? If you haven't, write a prayer in the space provided asking Jesus to come into your life. If you have already asked Jesus into your heart, write a letter thanking Him for what He did for you on the cross!

week 3

## "All Access Pass" Lanyard

Supplies Needed:

- 8.5 x 11" Colored Cardstock
- String or Ribbon
- Hole Punch
- Markers
- Stickers and Pretty Embellishments

Prep:

- Cut cardstock into four pieces
- Cut string or ribbon into lengths long enough to tie around each girl's neck with the lanyard.

What should I do?

Decorate the card with markers, stickers, etc. and write *All Access* on the card. Then write out John 14:6 on pretty paper and glue it on the back of the *All Access* card. Punch a hole in the top of the lanyard. Thread string or ribbon and tie.

## Activity Sheet

Romans 5:12 says, *"When Adam sinned, sin entered the world."* Draw a picture of Adam in the garden eating the apple that God told him not to eat.

**Polka Dot Girls ❃ Knowing God**

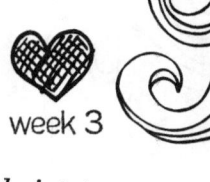
week 3

But Romans 5:8 says, *"But God showed His great love for us by sending Christ to die for us while we were still sinners."* Draw a picture of God sending Jesus to earth for us.

Romans 5 talks about how sin entered the world through the sin of Adam, and how Jesus coming provided a way for us to be forgiven of our sins. Read through Romans 5 in your Bible, and write out the following verses below.

Romans 5:12 _____

_____

_____

Romans 5:15 _____

_____

_____

Romans 5:16 _____

_____

_____

Romans 5:17 _____

_____

_____

Romans 5:18 _____

_____

_____

week 3

## Weekly Challenge

**Grow** – GROW your faith by reading about Jesus dying on the cross and coming back to life in Matthew 27 and 28.

**Love** – Maybe you have a friend or a family member that doesn't know what Jesus did for them on the cross. Tell them about Jesus today!

**Action** – Take ACTION: If you have asked Jesus to come into your heart, tell somebody about it! If you haven't asked Jesus into your heart, pray some more about this really important decision and ask God to help you know Him better.

**Memorize** – MEMORIZE the theme verse for this week:

*So now we can rejoice in our wonderful new relationship with God because our Lord Jesus Christ has made us friends of God.*
– Romans 5:11

# Knowing God

week 4

## God the Holy Spirit

### What's the point?

### Jesus sent us the Holy Spirit to be our comforter, teacher, and guide.

#### theme verse

*Then I will ask the Father to send you the Holy Spirit who will help you and always be with you.*
John 14:16 (CEV)

#### related bible story

Acts 2:1-4

Have you have ever played TAG? You chase everyone around the room, and when you finally touch someone what do you say? You say, "Tag, you're it!"

In the last chapter, we talked about Jesus coming to earth and dying on the cross to make a way for us have an All Access pass to God. When Jesus came to earth, he picked twelve people called the disciples to be his friends and to travel around with him while He taught them all the things they needed to know about God.

But after Jesus rose from the dead, He told the disciples that He was going to leave. He was going back to heaven. John 16:5 says, *"But now I am going away to the One who sent me."* Can you imagine how the disciples must have felt?

Have you ever have had a really good friend move away? Someone you really cared about who had helped you with a whole lot of things. When they told you they were leaving, how did you feel? You probably felt scared and worried and sad and lots of other things.

Well, the disciples felt exactly that way when Jesus told them that He was leaving earth and going back to heaven. But then Jesus told them something else really amazing. He said that He had to go away – but that He was going to send someone back to earth to be here with us forever. Do you know who that is? The Holy Spirit. Jesus had to leave, but when He left – He said "Tag, You're it!" to the Holy Spirit! Now it is the Holy Spirit's job to teach us and speak to us and show us all the things we need to know!

> John 15:26 says, "*I will send you the Spirit who comes from the Father and shows what is true. The Spirit will help you and will tell you about me.*" (CEV)

So Jesus went back up into heaven and a few days later the Holy Sprit came down to the disciples. Now, instead of Jesus teaching them all the things about God and helping them know what to do, the Holy Spirit would speak to them and guide them. And He is STILL here and will speak to you and me to help us know God better!

Now, the big difference is, the Holy Spirit doesn't have a human body like Jesus did. You can't see Him. You can't hear his voice with your ears like you can hear your teachers at school telling you things, but you can hear Him speak in your heart. Sometimes you will just have a feeling and that is the Holy Spirit whispering to you. We can't see Him with our eyes, but He is always with us.

### OH, I GET IT!

In some ways God is like a family with father, mother, and child - three persons and one family. Just remember that the Trinity does not mean that we have three gods. There is one God with three persons.

Polka Dot Girls ❧ Knowing God

The Bible talks about a few things specifically that the Holy Spirit does.

**First, the Holy Spirit is our:**

⇒ 1. Comforter

Do you have a blankie or a favorite stuffed animal from when you were really little? It's the special thing that when you're scared or sad or tired you like to hold on to and it helps you not be sad anymore? That special blanket or stuffed animal brings you COMFORT. It makes you feel better whenever you are upset.

And the Holy Spirit will bring you comfort too – just like your old blankie! 2 Corinthians 1:3-4 says, *"He is the compassionate Father and God of all comfort. He's the one who comforts us in all our trouble so that we can comfort other people who are in every kind of trouble."* (CEB)

Whenever you are scared or nervous or sad, the Holy Spirit will help you feel better. And you never have to leave Him at home like you have to do with your teddy bear. He is with you wherever you go, all the time! Say a prayer and ask Him to help you not to be upset and He will help you get through whatever it is you are facing.

**The second thing Holy Spirit promises to be for you, is your:**

⇒ 2. Teacher

Sarah *Loves* her teacher, Mrs. Crenshaw. She is the BEST teacher ever. She shows Sarah how to do all kinds of really cool things and helps her understand stuff that is hard to get. She is patient and is always willing to listen whenever Sarah has a question. She is really encouraging and always tells Sarah she's doing a good job.

But she also helps her in another way. Whenever Sarah has a spelling test, she hands it in to Mrs. Crenshaw and the teacher takes out a big red marker and circles all the words that Sarah got wrong. When Sarah sees the big red marks, she knows what she needs to work on and the things she needs to try harder at.

The Holy Spirit is a great teacher. He will show you all kinds of things about God. He will help you understand the Bible. He will help you know what Jesus wants you to do and how to live a life that makes God the Father happy. John 14:26 says,

> *"The Companion, the Holy Spirit, whom the Father will send in my name, will teach you everything and will remind you of everything I told you."* (CEB)

But the Holy Spirit will also help you know when you've done something wrong. How many of you have ever made a mistake or done something wrong and all of the sudden you get a feeling in your heart where you feel really bad about what you did? That is the Holy Spirit! He will draw big red circles around the things in your life that you need to change and areas of your behavior or attitude that don't make God happy. He shows us these things so we can learn to do better and make the right choices.

**And the last way the Holy Spirit will help you, is by being your:**

# ⇒ 3. Guide

Have you ever been lost? Have you ever looked around and realized you didn't know which way to go? Sometimes it's easy for us to get lost in our lives. We don't know what we should do. But the Holy Spirit promises to guide us!

Carrie had a big decision to make. She had been asked to join the traveling softball league for the summer, but if she joined the team, she knew that she would miss out on a lot of other activities she wanted to be a part of. She couldn't decide what to do! Her mom and dad told her that she could make the decision, but Carrie was torn. Although she loved playing softball, she was also interested in playing the piano and painting and even spending more time with her little sister. She needed help to know what to do.

So Carrie prayed. She asked God to help her know what to do. And one morning she woke up, and in her heart, she knew what her decision should be. It was so crazy! Nothing in particular happened, she just knew in her heart that she should pass on softball this year and spend time doing other things.

week 4

What changed? How did Carrie know what to do? Well, the Holy Spirit guided her into making the right decision. When she prayed, she was asking for His help, and so He gave her the answer she was looking for.

If you don't know what to do in a situation, why not stop and ask the Holy Spirit to guide you. Maybe you're not sure if you should say something. Ask the Holy Sprit if you should speak up or stay quiet. Maybe you're wondering if you should do something your friends are doing. The Holy Spirit will speak to you and help you know what the right thing is – AND He will give you the courage to do the right thing too!

Psalm 143:10 says, "*Teach me to do your will, for you are my God. May your gracious Spirit lead me forward on a firm footing.*" God will guide you. The Holy Spirit will speak to you and help you know where to go, what to say, and how to act.

Aren't you glad that Jesus sent us the Holy Spirit! I'm so thankful that when Jesus left, He didn't leave us all on earth alone with no one to show what to do. I'm glad he "tagged" the Holy Spirit to come down to earth to be our comforter, our teacher, and our guide.

**Closing Prayer:** *Dear God, Thank you for sending the Holy Spirit to help me. Thank you that I can know that He will comfort me when I'm sad, that He will teach me things about you, and guide me into making the right choices in my life. Help me to know His voice. Amen.*

The Holy Spirit came to earth when Jesus left. Have you ever had a friend move away? How did you feel when your friend left? How do you think the disciples felt when Jesus left the earth?

Jesus told His disciples that He would not leave them alone – but that He would send someone to take His place on the earth. Who is that person?

Look up John 14:16 in your Bible and write it out here:

Polka Dot Girls ❧ Knowing God

week 4

What does the word COMFORTER mean?

Think of some things that COMFORT you! Write them out (or draw a picture) next to the blankie!

What are some ways the Holy Spirit comforts us?

The Holy Spirit is also our TEACHER. Who is your FAVORITE teacher and why?

How does a teacher help you?

week 4

The list below shows some of the ways the Holy Spirit teaches us. Put a check mark next to the things that the Holy Spirit has taught you!

- ☐ He will teach you about Jesus
- ☐ He will help you understand the Bible
- ☐ He will help you know when you've done something wrong.
- ☐ He will remind you of things you have learned.
- ☐ He will tell you to help other people.
- ☐ He will give you courage to tell others about Jesus.

The Holy Spirit will also be our guide. Have you ever had a time when you didn't know what to do in a situation? Write out your experience here.

Is there something the Holy Spirit it asking you to do right now? Take a minute and ask Him to show you something He would like you to do. Listen carefully and then write out what He speaks to your heart in the space provided.

week 4

## Kool Comfort Pad!

<u>Supplies Needed:</u>

- Old or New White Tube Sock
- Fabric Markers
- Thin tipped permanent markers
- Rice (not instant rice)
- Ribbon

<u>What should I do?</u>

- Decorate your white tube sock with your favorite color fabric markers. (Draw pictures and/or write today's verse on the sock)
- Fill the tube sock ¾ full with rice.
- Tie the top of the tube sock with pretty ribbon. Double knot the ribbon so the rice does not fall out of the sock.
- Warm in microwave and enjoy!

    Place the rice-filled sock in your microwave oven for 2 to 3 minutes on high power. Time may vary by microwave.

    Remove the sock from the microwave and place where you need comfort.

## Activity Sheet

Solve the puzzle by substituting the numbers for the letters.

| 1 | 2 | 3 | 4 | 5 | 6 | 7 | 8 | 9 | 10 | 11 | 12 | 13 | 14 | 15 |
|---|---|---|---|---|---|---|---|---|----|----|----|----|----|----|
| A | Q | I | P | F | V | X | N | Y | D  | W  | Z  | K  | S  | G  |

| 16 | 17 | 18 | 19 | 20 | 21 | 22 | 23 | 24 | 25 | 26 |
|----|----|----|----|----|----|----|----|----|----|----|
| O  | U  | R  | C  | E  | M  | H  | T  | L  | J  | B  |

__ __ __ __ __   __ __ __   __ __ __
3  11 3  24 24   1  14 13   23 22 20

__ __ __ __ __ __ .  __ __ __   __ __
5  1 23 22 20 18    1  8 10    22 20

__ __ __ __   __ __ __ __   __ __ __
11 3 24 24    15 3 6 20     9 16 17

__ __ __ __ __ __ __   __ __ __ __ __
1 8 16 23 22 20 18    5 18 3 20 8 10

__ __   __ __ __ __   __ __ __   __ __ __
23 16   22 20 24 4    9 16 17    1 8 10

__ __   __ __ __   __ __ __ __ __   __ __ __
23 16   26 20      11 3 23 22       9 16 17

14:16 NIV

__ __ __ __ __ __ __ .  __ __ __ __ __
5 16 18 20 6 20 18      25 16 22 8

Polka Dot Girls ❀ Knowing God

week 4

Look up each scripture in the Bible and fill in the blank.

*But you will receive _____ when the Holy Spirit comes on you; and you will be my witnesses in Jerusalem, and in Judea and Samaria, and to the ends of the earth.* – Acts 1:8

*³Give _____ to the God and Father of our Lord Jesus Christ! He is the Father who gives tender love. All comfort comes from him. ⁴He _____ us in all our troubles. Now we can comfort others when they are in trouble. We ourselves have received comfort from God.* – 2 Corinthians 1:3-4

*I will send the _____ to you from the Father. He is the Spirit of truth, who comes out from the Father. When the Friend comes to _____ you, he will give witness about me.* – John 15:26

*I baptize you with water, but he will baptize you with the _____.* – Mark 1:8

*The angel answered, 'The Holy Spirit will come on you, and the _____ of the Most High will overshadow you. So the holy one to be born will be called the Son of God'.* – Luke 1:35

*May the God of hope fill you with all _____ and _____ as you trust in him, so that you may overflow with hope by the power of the Holy Spirit.* – Romans 15:13

*But the _____ of the Spirit is love, joy, peace, forbearance, kindness, goodness, faithfulness, gentleness and self-control. Against such things there is no law.* – Galatians 5:22, 23

*You _____ me with your counsel.* – Psalm 73:24

*But the _____ , the Holy Spirit, whom the Father will send in my name, will _____ you all things and will remind you of everything I have said to you.* – John 14:26

<sup>10</sup> *Just as Jesus was coming up out of the _____, he saw heaven being torn open and the _____ descending on him like a dove.* <sup>11</sup> *And a voice came from heaven: "You are my _____, whom I love; with you I am well pleased.* – Mark 1:10, 11

week 4

# Weekly Challenge

**Grow** – GROW your faith by reading about how Jesus sent the Holy Spirit to help comfort, teach and guide us in John 14:15-27.

**Love** – If someone in your family is feeling sad, lonely or afraid, give them your favorite blanket or stuffed toy and tell them about the Holy Spirit.

**Act** – Take ACTION: Pray to the Holy Spirit and ask Him for guidance when you have to make a choice or a decision. Be sure to try to listen for his voice. You can do it!

**Memorize** – MEMORIZE the theme verse for this week:

*Then I will ask the Father to send you the Holy Spirit who will help you and always be with you.*
– John 14:16 CEV

www.ingramcontent.com/pod-product-compliance
Lightning Source LLC
Chambersburg PA
CBHW060518300426

44112CB00017B/2724